BIG RED BATH

To Theo William and Maya Josephine — J.J.
For Rebecca Anne — A.R.

ORCHARD BOOKS
Carmelite House, 50 Victoria Embankment, London EC4Y 0DZ
Orchard Books Australia
Level 17/207 Kent Street, Sydney, NSW 2000
First published in 2004 by Orchard Books
First published in paperback in 2005
ISBN 978 1 40835 602 9
Text © Julia Jarman 2004
Illustrations © Adrian Reynolds 2004
The rights of Julia Jarman to be identified as the author
and Adrian Reynolds to be identified as the illustrator
of this work have been asserted by them in accordance
with the Copyright, Designs and Patents Act, 1988.
A CIP catalogue record for this book is available from the British Library.
10
Printed in China
Orchard Books is a division of Hachette Children's Books,
an Hachette UK Company.
www.hachette.co.uk

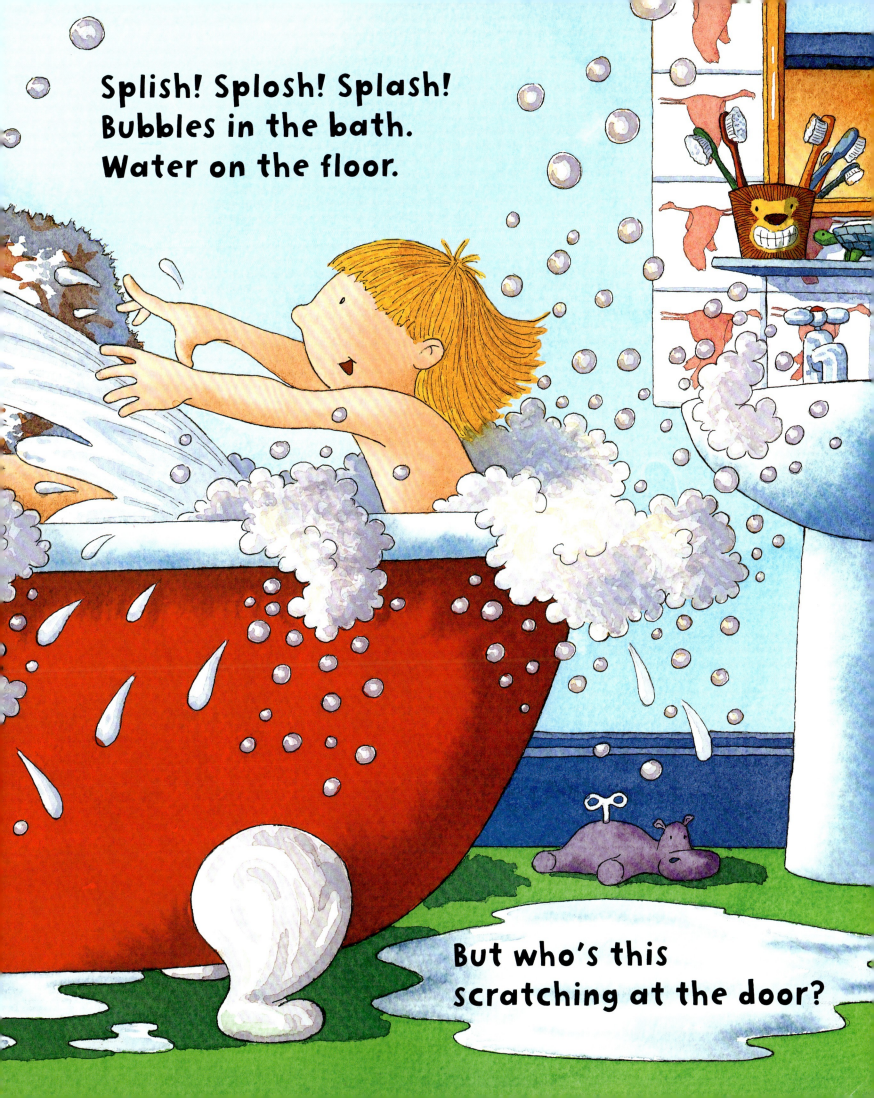

"Hi there, kids! Can I come for a swim?"
"Course you can, Dog. Just dive in!"

Dog dives in, front feet first.

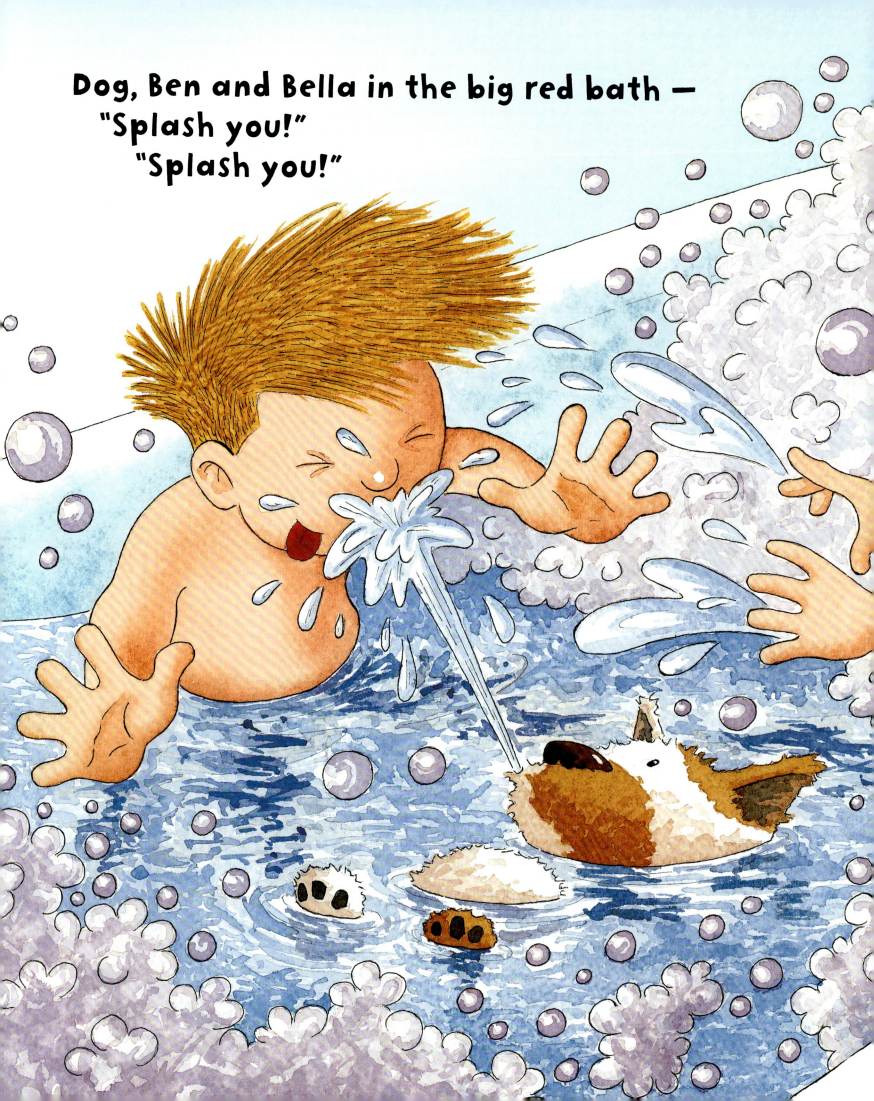

"Hi there, kids! Can I have a wash?"
"Leap in, Lion. Splish and splosh!"

Lion leaps in and starts to scrub.

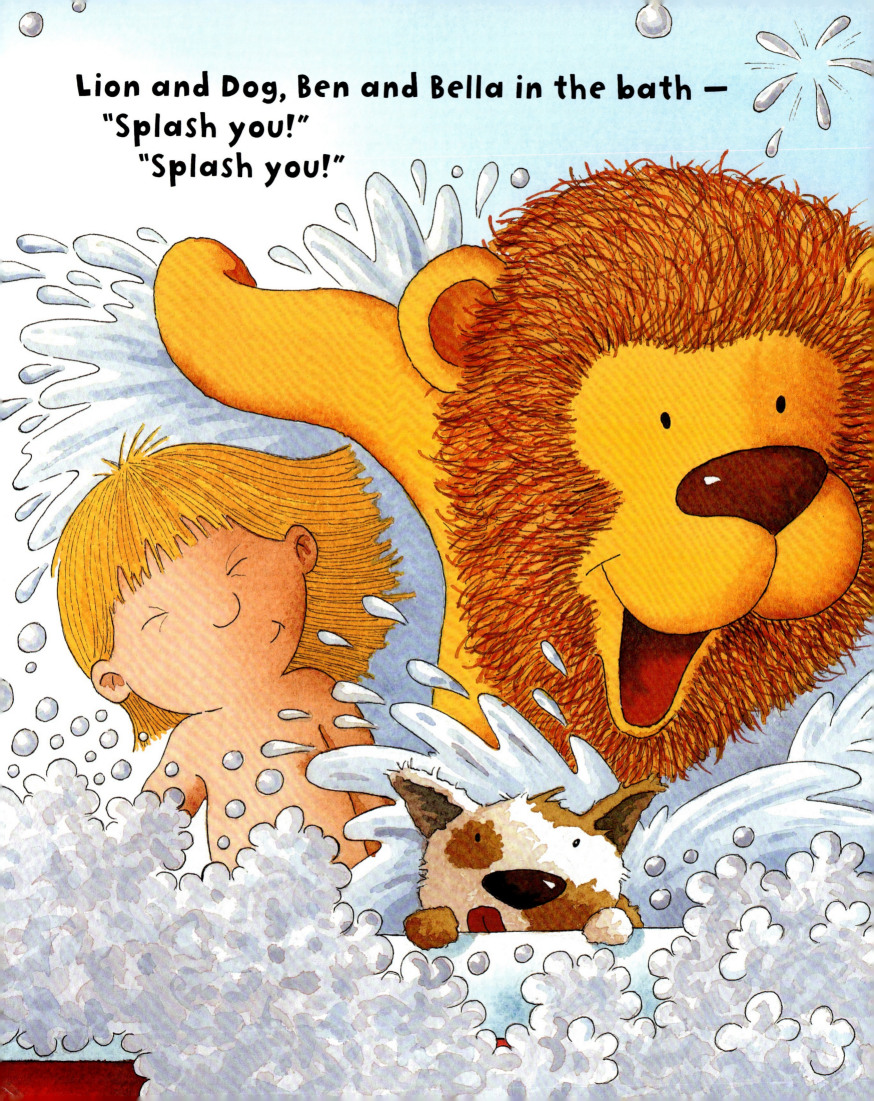

Lion and Dog, Ben and Bella in the bath —
"Splash you!"
"Splash you!"

"Hello, kids! Can I come for a paddle?"
"Course you can, Duck! Dibble and dabble!"

Duck dibble-dabbles at a quacking pace.

He slides under the bath —

which goes

sloosh

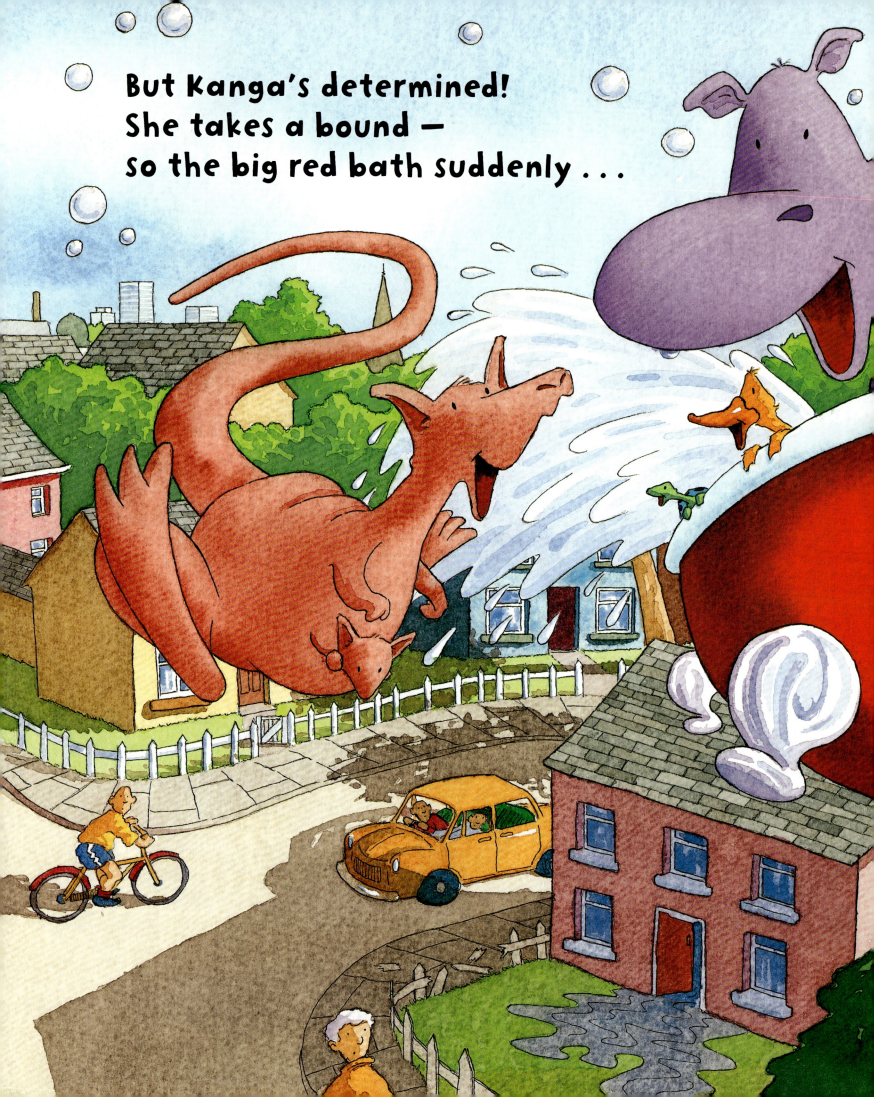

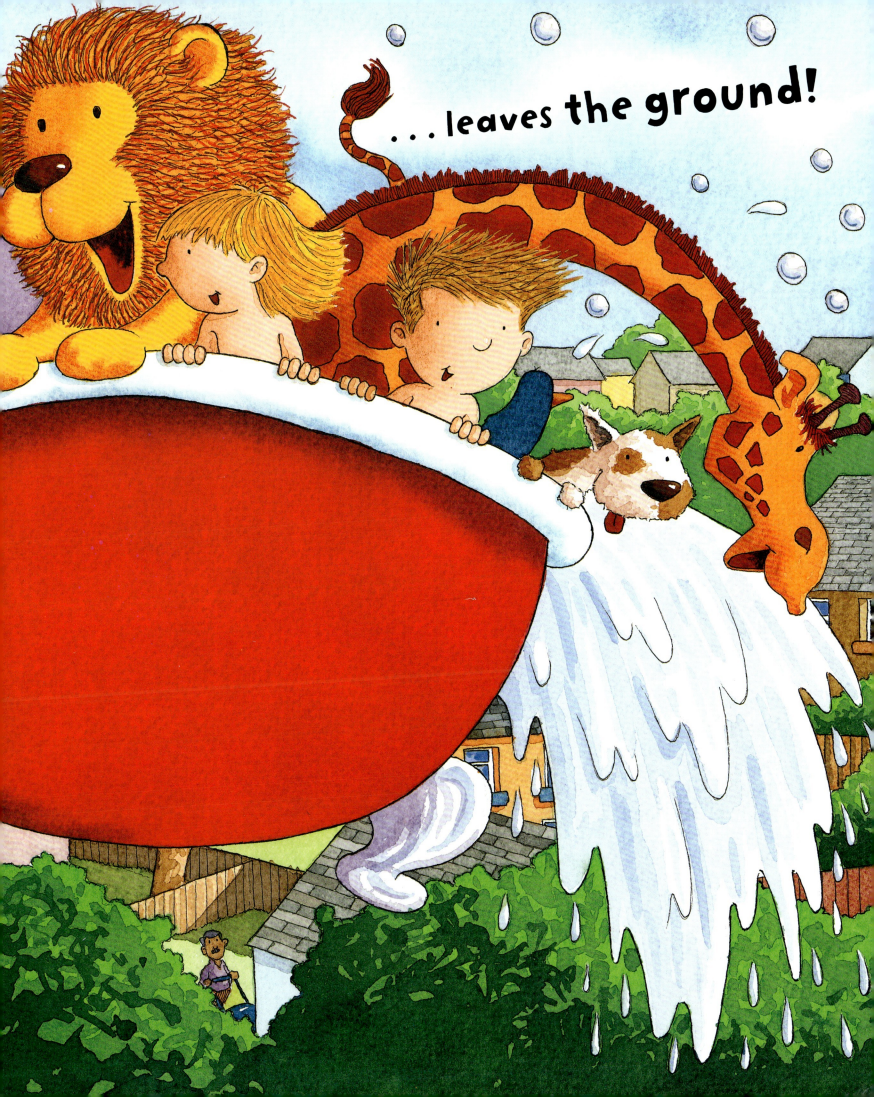

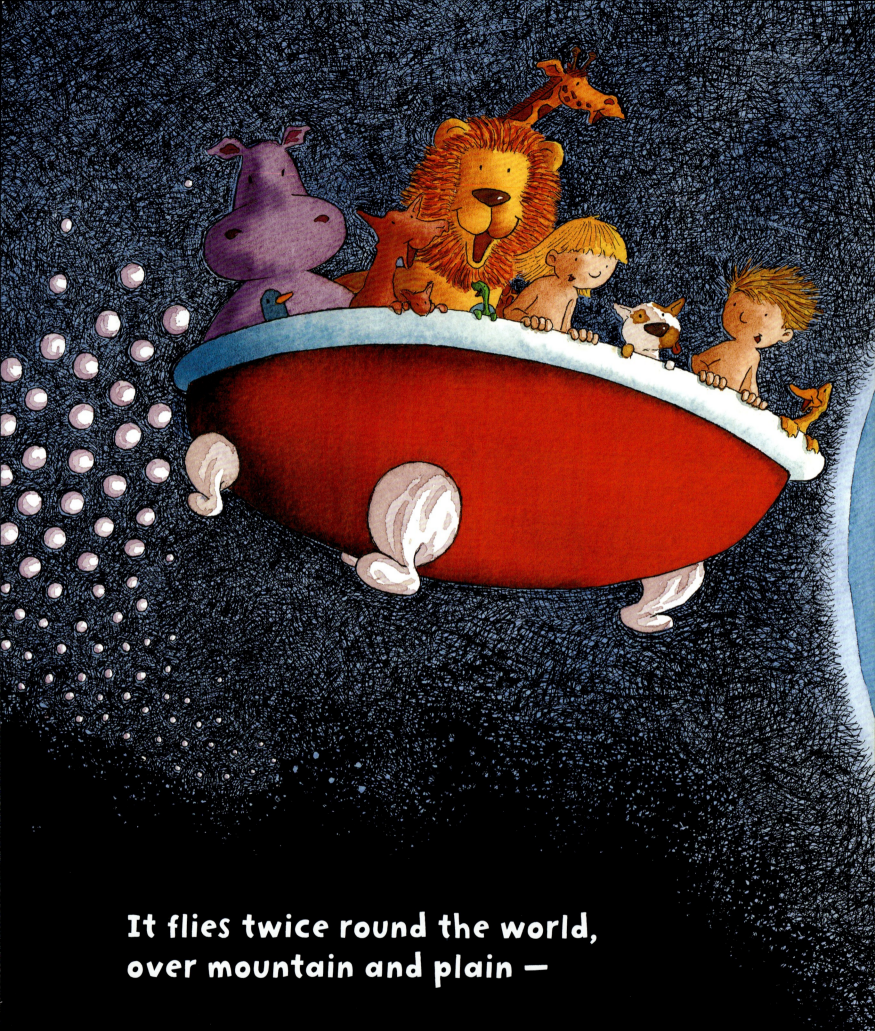

It flies twice round the world,
over mountain and plain —

till a flock of flamingos...

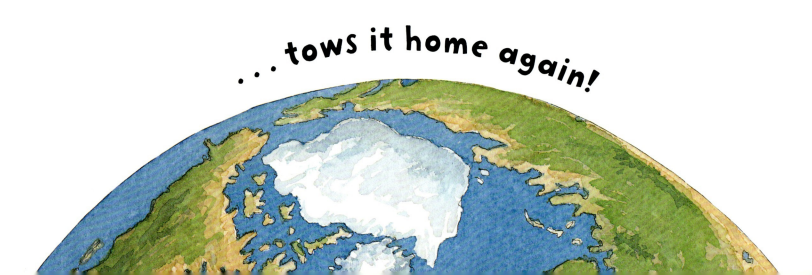

...tows it home again!